W9-CMI-805

Crickets

by Emily K. Green

BELLWETHER MEDIA • MINNEAPOLIS, MN

BLASTOFF!
2
READERS

Note to Librarians, Teachers, and Parents:

Blastoff! Readers are carefully developed by literacy experts and combine standards-based content with developmentally appropriate text.

Level 1 provides the most support through repetition of high-frequency words, light text, predictable sentence patterns, and strong visual support.

Level 2 offers early readers a bit more challenge through varied simple sentences, increased text load, and less repetition of high-frequency words.

Level 3 advances early-fluent readers toward fluency through increased text and concept load, less reliance on visuals, longer sentences, and more literary language.

Whichever book is right for your reader, Blastoff! Readers are the perfect books to build confidence and encourage a love of reading that will last a lifetime!

This edition first published in 2007 by Bellwether Media.

Library of Congress Cataloging-in-Publication Data
Green, Emily K., 1966–
 Crickets / by Emily K. Green.
  p. cm. — (Blastoff! readers) (World of insects)
Summary: "Simple text accompanied by full-color photographs give an up-close look at crickets."
 Includes bibliographical references and index.
 ISBN-10: 1-60014-011-4 (hardcover : alk. paper)
 ISBN-13: 978-1-60014-011-2 (hardcover : alk. paper)
 1. Crickets—Juvenile literature. I. Title. II. Series.

QL508.G8G74 2006
595.7'26–dc22   2006001994

Table of Contents

Crickets are **insects**
that sing.

Crickets can be brown,
black, or green.

Most crickets hide in the grass or under rocks in the day. They come out at night.

6

Some kinds of crickets live
under the ground.

All crickets have six legs.

Their back legs have
strong muscles.

Crickets jump with their
back legs. Crickets can
jump very high and far.

10

Most crickets have ears on
their legs. They listen for
other crickets.

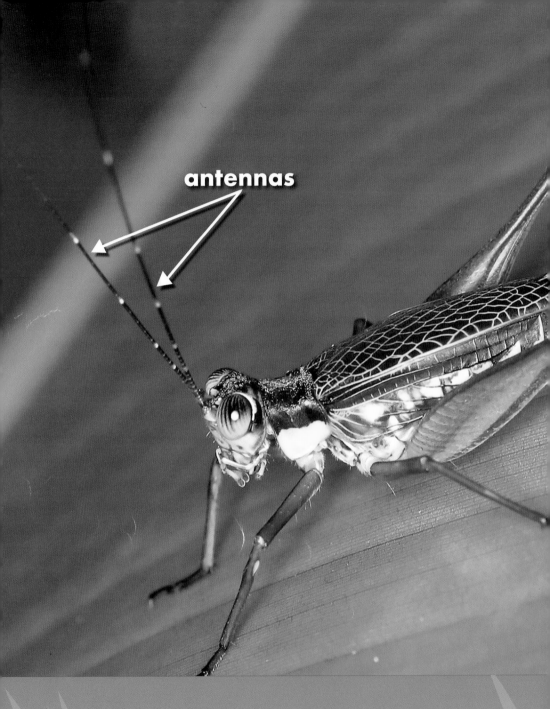

antennas

Crickets have **antennas**.

Crickets use their antennas
to touch and smell.

Crickets have **cerci**. Cerci
are short feelers on the back
of a cricket's body.

14

Cerci

Crickets use their cerci to sense danger.

Birds, snakes, spiders and lizards eat crickets. That's danger!

Most crickets have wings that lie flat on their backs.

Some crickets use their wings to fly. Most crickets do not fly.

Crickets rub their wings
together to sing.

Every kind of cricket has a different song.

Crickets follow the songs to find a **mate**. Have you ever heard a cricket sing?

21

Glossary

antennas—the long, thin feelers on an insect's head; crickets use the feelers to look for food.

cerci—the short, pointy feelers at the back of the cricket's body; crickets sense air movement with their cerci.

insect—a kind of animal that has a hard body; most insects also have two antennas, six legs, and two or four wings.

mate—one of a pair of animals; insects find another insect to have young.

To Learn More

AT THE LIBRARY

Bunting, Eve. *Christmas Cricket*. New York: Clarion Books, 2002.

Carle, Eric. *The Very Quiet Cricket*. New York: Philomel Books, 1990.

Caudill, Rebecca. *A Pocketful of Cricket*. New York: Holt, Rinehart and Winston, 1964.

Wheeler, Lisa. *Old Cricket*. New York: Atheneum Books, 2003.

ON THE WEB

Learning more about crickets is as easy as 1, 2, 3.

1. Go to www.factsurfer.com

2. Enter "crickets" into search box.

3. Click the "Surf" button and you will see a list of related web sites.

With factsurfer.com, finding more information is just a click away.

Index

The photographs in this book are reproduced through the courtesy of: blickwinkel/Alamy, front cover; Graphic Science/Alamy, p. 4; JH Pete Carmichael/Getty Images, p. 5; Simone Vanden Berg, p. 6; Roger Eritja/Alamy, p. 7; Photolibrarycom/Getty Images, p. 8; neil hardwick/Alamy, p. 9; Heintje Joseph T. Lee, pp. 10-11; Christopher Tan Teck Hean, pp. 12-13; canismaior, pp. 14-15; ljuco, p. 15(inset); William Radcliffe/Getty Images, p. 16; pixelman, p. 17; John Brackenbury/Alamy, p. 18; Peter Lilja/Getty Images, p. 19; Goh Mea How, pp. 20-21.